Dear Rosie

Written by Eugenie Marler
Illustrated by Pat Reynolds

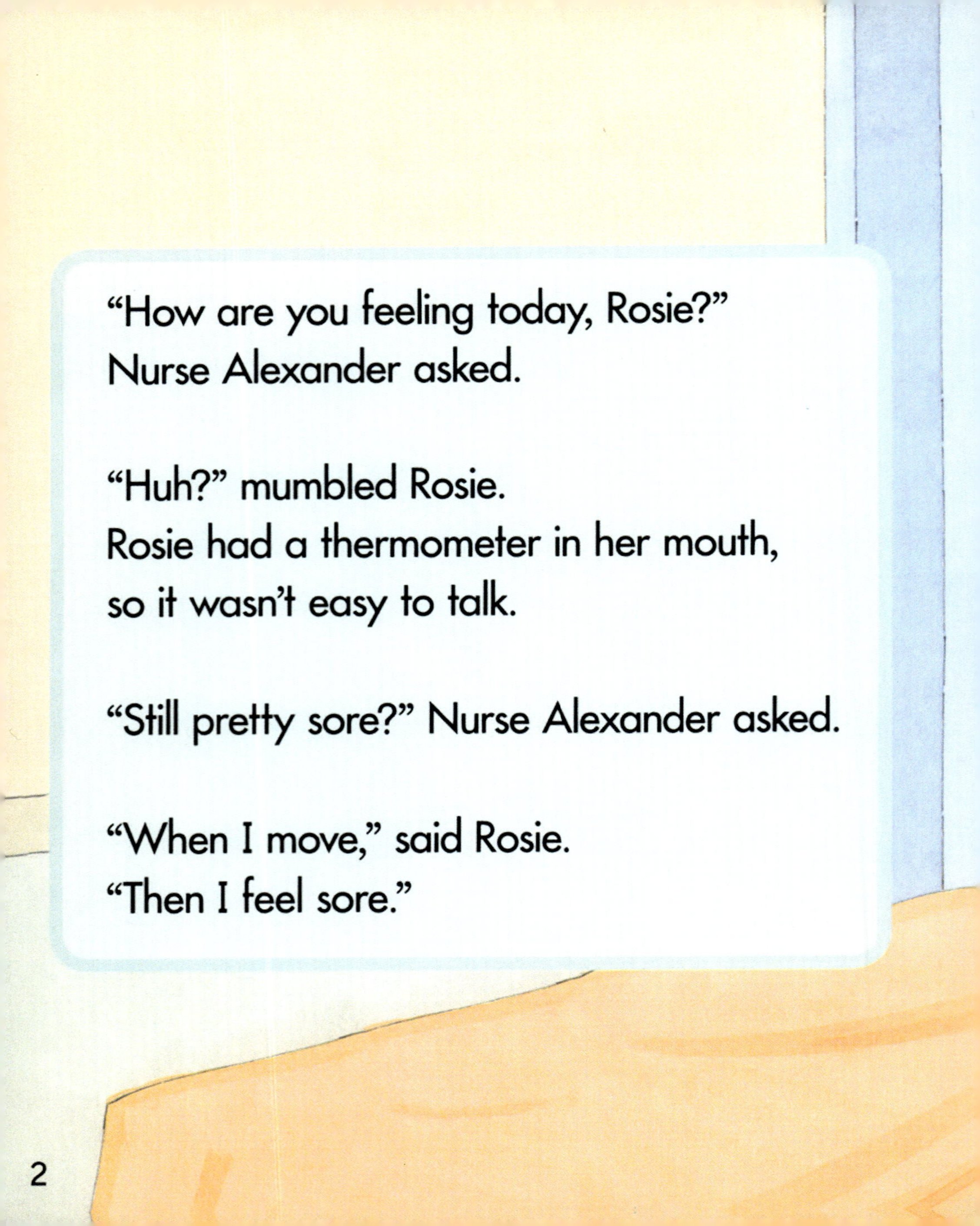

"How are you feeling today, Rosie?"
Nurse Alexander asked.

"Huh?" mumbled Rosie.
Rosie had a thermometer in her mouth,
so it wasn't easy to talk.

"Still pretty sore?" Nurse Alexander asked.

"When I move," said Rosie.
"Then I feel sore."

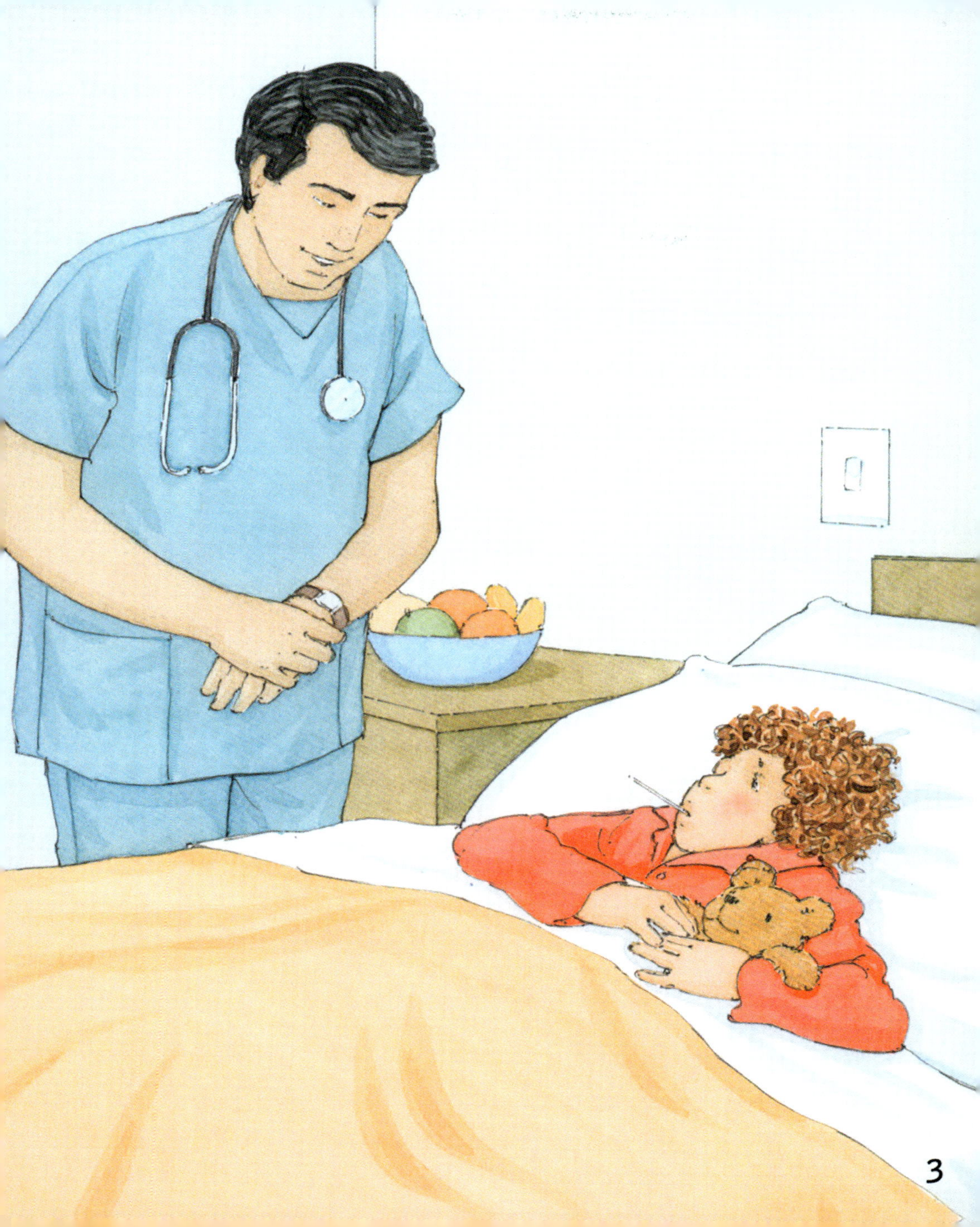

Nurse Alexander looked at Rosie's chart, then drew a line on it.

"If you move early, you'll get better sooner," said Nurse Alexander.
"I'll help you, so you'll walk a little better."

"I've had an operation, though, so it's sore!" cried Rosie.

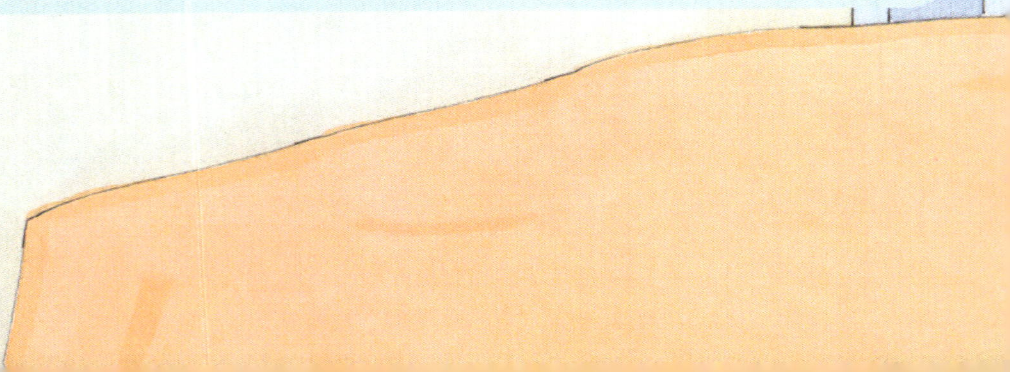

"You can do it, Rosie," Nurse Alexander said,
helping Rosie sit upright.
"If you walk now, it won't be so sore next time.
If you try and walk,
I'll give you a surprise when we get back."

"What surprise?" Rosie asked.

"Walk first, then surprise,"
answered Nurse Alexander.

"I hope it's a nice surprise," Rosie muttered.

"Looks like somebody has dropped you a line," said Nurse Alexander.

"What does that mean?" asked Rosie.

"It means somebody has written you a letter," replied Nurse Alexander.
"All these letters are for you.
People have written letters
so you will feel better."

"Six of my school friends have written letters!" said Rosie.
"That makes me feel better already."

“They have all written letters because they are good friends,” said Nurse Alexander, smiling.

The first letter Rosie opened was from Francesca.

Dear Rosie

I hear you've had your appendix out,
so I bet you're in pain.
It was too bad
you couldn't come with us to camp
because you had to go to hospital.

We're all thinking of you.

From
Francesca

Dear Rosie

Today at camp,
we went over a river on a flying fox.
I was terrified!
Jonathan didn't hold on
to the line properly, so he fell in.
Luckily, he can swim!

Get well soon!

From
Felicity

Dear Rosie

I heard you were sick,
so I thought I'd drop you a line
from camp.

Every day, we do fun things outdoors,
so we never get bored.

Everybody has to help with meals,
so tomorrow I'll be drying the dishes.
Just my luck!

Hope you're feeling better.

From
Isabella

Dear Rosie

You can't be with us,
so we miss you very much.
If you were here,
we'd have even more fun
at camp.

Tomorrow, we're going hiking
up a mountain.

Take care of yourself
and get well soon!

From
Jacqueline

Dear Rosie

We're having a brilliant time at camp.
Poor you, stuck in a boring hospital!

Yesterday, we went fishing.
I caught six guppies!
They were too little to eat,
so I threw all six back again.

Tomorrow, we are going back home.
It's too soon!

From
Belinda

Dear Rosie

Yesterday, we had a massive bonfire.
We cooked sausages
and marshmallows on sticks.
My sausage was too hot.
It burned my tongue – yow!
I had to have a cold drink.
That stopped it hurting.

The day after tomorrow,
I'll come and visit you in hospital.
Mum says because you are sick
I can bring you some grapes.

From
Michaela

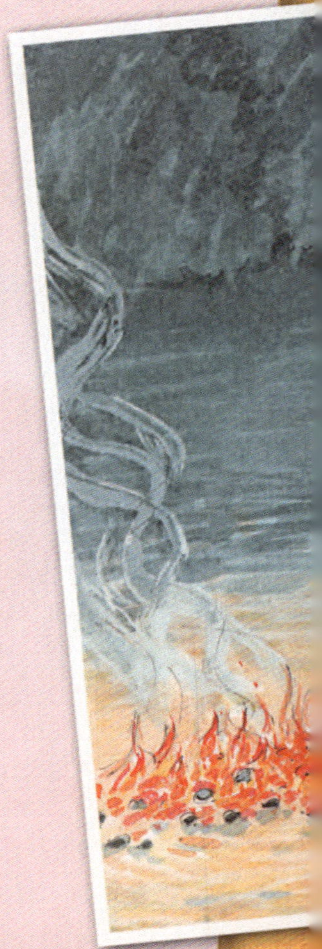

Rosie looked at the date on the letter.

"The day after tomorrow –
that's today!" she said.

There was a knock on the door.
"Here we are!" six friends yelled.